T0042536

SCHIRMER'S LIBRARY
OF MUSICAL CLASSICS

Vol. 1932

ANTONIN DVOŘÁK

Op. 100

Sonatina

For Violin and Piano

Violin part edited by Rok Klopčič

ISBN 978-0-7935-6414-9

G. SCHIRMER, Inc.

DISTRIBUTED BY

HAL•LEONARD®
CORPORATION
7777 W. BLUEMOUND RD. P.O. BOX 13819 MILWAUKEE, WI 53213

Copyright © 1979 by G. Schirmer, Inc. (ASCAP) New York, NY
International Copyright Secured. All Rights Reserved.
**Warning: Unauthorized reproduction of this publication is
prohibited by Federal law and subject to criminal prosecution.**

Foreword

Antonín Dvořák (1841-1904) completed his Sonatina for violin and piano Opus 100, on December 3, 1893 in New York. For this edition two publications were used: the first edition, published by Simrock in 1894, and the edition from the series *Kritické vydání podle skladatelova rukopisu* (critical edition after the composer's manuscript) published by the Antonín Dvořák Society in 1955 in Prague.

The violin and piano part of this edition is based on a comparison of these two editions. I have tried to find the best possible solution to the discrepancies between them. A few more differences should be noted:

> Movement II: Measures 9-16 are written with the sign 8ª······· (ad libitum) in the autograph. Measure 72, the *Meno. Tempo I,* is taken from the autograph. Simrock gives this indication at measure 56, and none at all in measure 72.

> Movement IV: The tempo indication at the beginning of this movement is given in the autograph as *Allegro molto.*

The separate violin part is the editor's version. Some suggestions for the articulation are given. These are taken from the separate violin part of the Simrock edition, which sometimes differs from the violin part in the piano score of the same edition. A few obviously missing signs added by the editor are in brackets.

R.K.

SONATINA

Violin part edited by Rok Klopčič

Antonín Dvořák, Op. 100

I

II

Poco più mosso.

Meno Tempo I

Violin

SONATINA

Violin part edited by Rok Klopčič

Antonin Dvořák, Op. 100

I

Allegro risoluto

48176cx

Violin

Violin

II

Violin
III
SCHERZO

Violin

Violin

Violin

III

SCHERZO

IV

FINALE